TriPickaty Academy
Presents

Bluegrass Music
Beware: Addictively Fun

All Sorts of Bluegrass Trivia and Games

For serious (and not-so serious) bluegrass fans.

Expand your bluegrass knowledge.

Finger picking fun.

By: Kathleen McMahon

ISBN-13: 978-1985673571 (CreateSpace-Assigned)
ISBN-10: 1985673576

BISAC: Music / Genres & Styles / Folk & Traditional

Copyright © 2018 by Applied Communications, LLC

First Edition

All rights reserved. No part of this book may be used or reproduced in any manner whatsoever without prior written permission of the author/publisher, except in the case of brief quotations embodied in reviews.

Contact:
tripickaty@gmail.com
151 Wedgewood Ln.
Whitefish, MT 59937

Table of Contents

My Bluegrass Profile	1
Bluegrass Timeline	2
Bluegrass Word Search	4
Bill Monroe Trivia	5
Bluegrass Tidbits	7
Circle of Fifths	8
I Learned About Life in a Bluegrass Jam	9
Bluegrass Word Scramble	10
Bluegrass Fitness	11
Test Your Bluegrass Knowledge	12
Bluegrass vs. Old Time Music	14
Nine Movies with Banjo Music	16
Bluegrass Match Game	17
How Well Do You Know Your Train Songs?	18
Best Bluegrass Dog Names	19
Practice Tips for Bluegrass Musicians	20
What is Your Bluegrass Band Name?	22
Bluegrass and Jazz	23
Bluegrass Song Challenge	24
Did You Know?	25
Pick Your Next Jam Song	26
Bluegrass Festival Scavenger Hunt	28

Table of Contents (cont.)

Bluegrass Music is Good for You	29
Top Bluegrass Cat Names	30
Guess Who?	31
A Day at the Museum	32
Bluegrass Words	34
People You Didn't Know Played the Banjo	35
Bluegrass Bucket List	36
Bluegrass and Celtic Music	37
Bluegrass Charades	38
Bluegrass License Plate Bingo	39
Promote Bluegrass Music	40
Make Your Own Banjo Jokes	41
Bluegrass Show and Tell	42
Bluegrass Festival Log	43
A Year of Bluegrass	44
Bluegrass Recipe – Jam-balaya	46
Bluegrass Song List	47
Answers	50

My Bluegrass Profile

Name:	
Address:	
I play these instruments:	
Favorite bluegrass songs:	
First bluegrass festival I attended:	
Favorite bluegrass festival:	
Favorite bluegrass music camp:	
Favorite bluegrass bands:	
Favorite bluegrass memory:	

Bluegrass Timeline

1920's
*Carter Family makes first recording. Many of their songs become bluegrass standards.

1930's
*The Monroe Brothers move to Chicago and play on the WLS radio show, "National Barn Dance".
* Bill Monroe forms his own group. Bill Monroe & the Blue Grass Boys first play on Grand Ole Opry in 1939.

1940's
*Bill Monroe & the Blue Grass Boys make their first record. Lester Flat & Earl Scruggs join the Bluegrass Boys.
*The Stanley Brothers make their first record.

1950's
*The term "Bluegrass", now in popular use, begins to describe a specific music genre.
*Elvis Presley records Bill Monroe classic, "Blue Moon of Kentucky", in 4/4 time.

1960's
*The first bluegrass festival is held in Roanke, VA.
*_Bluegrass Unlimited Magazine_ begins publishing (in 1966).
*Bluegrass soundtrack for movie _Bonnie & Clyde_ features the song "Foggy Mountain Breakdown".

Bluegrass Timeline (cont.)

1970's
- The movie *Deliverance* is released in 1972 with "Dueling Banjos" in the sound track.
- Nitty Gritty Dirt Band releases "Will The Circle Be Unbroken" album and introduces new fans to bluegrass music.
- New grass sparks debate about what constitutes bluegrass music.

1980's
- National Academy of Recording Arts & Sciences awards a Grammy for the first time in the category of "Bluegrass Album" to Bill Monroe.
- *Bluegrass, A History*, by Neil Rosenberg, is published by University of Illinois Press.

1990's
- Alison Krauss wins her first grammy for "Bluegrass Recording". She eventually becomes the top grammy winner of all time with 27 wins.
- International Bluegrass Music Association inducts first Hall of Fame members (Bill Monroe, Lester Flatt & Earl Scruggs).

2000's
- *O Brother Where Art Thou* movie released in 2000 featuring several bluegrass artists. Soundtrack had sold almost 8 million copies by 2015.
- Satellite radio launches all "Bluegrass" channel. Along with Internet streaming, bluegrass music is now available 24/7.

2010's
- PBS airs documentary, *Give Me the Banjo*, narrated by Steve Martin.
- The book *Pretty Good for a Girl*, by Murphy Hicks Henry, is released. The book chronicles women's contribution to bluegrass

Bluegrass Word Search

(See back of book for answers.)

Q	S	C	W	E	G	R	L	I	C	K	T
B	Z	B	A	N	D	U	Y	U	I	O	P
R	X	F	T	Y	H	M	I	K	J	A	M
E	F	I	D	D	L	E	O	T	P	L	M
A	A	S	M	O	N	R	O	E	A	T	U
K	B	G	H	N	U	J	M	L	W	R	Y
B	N	L	M	F	E	S	T	I	V	A	L
O	L	L	U	T	R	A	D	O	B	R	O
N	P	O	A	E	S	B	O	E	R	H	B
P	I	M	C	W	G	E	N	R	T	O	A
I	L	U	L	K	I	R	A	M	A	M	N
C	M	S	O	H	T	T	A	R	K	A	J
K	A	I	S	M	B	A	S	S	M	M	O
G	K	C	R	A	L	C	N	O	S	H	A
R	A	D	M	A	N	D	O	L	I	N	y

Word List

BAND	BANJO	BASS	BLUEGRASS
BREAK	DOBRO	FESTIVAL	FIDDLE
PICK	GUITAR	JAM	LICK
MANDOLIN	MONROE	MUSIC	

Bill Monroe Trivia

Test your knowledge of this bluegrass icon.
(See back of book for answers.)

1. Bill Monroe originally played in a band called the "The Monroe Brothers." What was his brother's name?
   - a. Fred
   - b. Charlie
   - c. Jimmy
   - d. Larry

2. Where was Bill Monroe born?
   - a. Rosine, KY
   - b. Lexington, KY
   - c. Owensboro, KY
   - d. Mount Olive, NC

3. What year did Bill Monroe start his band "Bill Monroe and the Blue Grass Boys"?
   - a. 1932
   - b. 1935
   - c. 1937
   - d. 1939

4. What was the first single that Bill Monroe and the Blue Grass Boys recorded?
   - a. Darling Corey
   - b. Mule Skinner Blues
   - c. Bluegrass Breakdown
   - d. Can't You Hear me Callin?

5. Which person was **NOT** at one time a member of the Blue Grass Boys?
   - a. Howdy Forrester
   - b. Chubby Wise
   - c. Slim Pickens
   - d. Curly Bradshaw

6. Who was the first Blue Grass Boy banjo player?
   - a. Earl Scruggs
   - b. Don Reno
   - c. String Bean
   - d. Sonny Osborne

7. In the 1940s, Bill Monroe and the Blue Grass Boys, along with their road crew, also played as a baseball team. They had their own uniforms and would compete against local semi-pro teams.

   True   False

Bill Monroe Trivia (cont.)

8. What was the first song that Bill Monroe recorded that was his own composition?
   a. Cry, Cry My Darling
   b. My Rose of Old Kentucky
   c. Kentucky Waltz
   d. Toy Heart

9. Who was the first person to start playing with Bill Monroe and the Blue Grass Boys?
   a. Lester Flatt
   b. Earl Scruggs
   c. Jimmy Martin
   d. Tom Ewing

10. At times, Bill Monroe had an accordion player accompany the Blue Grass Boys?

    True   False

11. Which President awarded Bill Monroe the National Medal of the Arts?
    a. Ronald Reagan
    b. Jimmy Carter
    c. George W. Bush
    d. Bill Clinton

12. Which song was **NOT** written by Bill Monroe?
    a. Blue Moon of Kentucky
    b. Footprints in the Snow
    c. Uncle Pen
    d. Little Georgia Rose

13. Who was the female band member who played with Bill Monroe and the Blue Grass Boys during the 1940's?
    a. Margie Sullivan
    b. Sally Ann Forrester
    c. Wilma Lee Cooper
    d. Rose Maddox

14. What was the name of Bill's Monroe's horse?
    a. Silver
    b. Mr. Ed
    c. King Wilkie
    d. Wildfire

Bluegrass Tidbits

The Bluegrass Style

"The bluegrass style depends upon a common musical vocabulary. It is a kind of language that is necessarily spoken in jam sessions made up of players who were strangers just a moment ago. Musical styles get passed back and forth in jam sessions. In a way, without jam sessions and the army of amateurs that play in them, there would be no recognizable style of music called bluegrass"

Source: International Bluegrass Music Museum

Bluegrass Math

Bluegrass Humor

Q: What is the difference between a bluegrass musician and a savings bond?

A: Eventually, a savings bond will mature and earn money.

Circle of Fifths

For those who are unfamiliar with the diagram below, this circle is a powerful decoding device which reveals the secrets of chord progressions, changing keys and all sorts of wonders to take your music playing and song writing to new levels. Below is a simplified explanation to help you begin to unlock the mysteries of this magical musical tool.

Many bluegrass songs have a common chord progression that is referred to as a "1-4-5". To find the 1-4-5 chords, locate the key of the song on the circle. This is the "1st" chord. The letter to the left of the "1st" chord is the "4th" chord and the letter to the right is the "5th" chord. For example, in the key of "G", the 1-4-5 chords are: G-C-D.

For more on the music theory behind the circle, you'll have to search the Internet. BUT, if you memorize this diagram, you will become the "Master of the Jam."

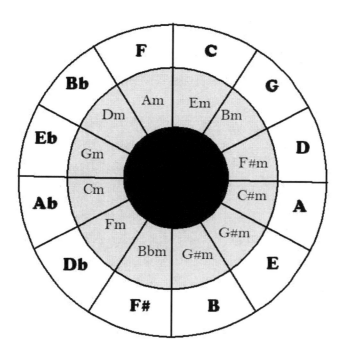

I Learned About Life in a Bluegrass Jam

1. Take turns.

2. Don't play too loud.

3. It's more fun to play with other people than to play alone.

4. You get better with practice.

5. Help out and encourage newcomers.

6. You play better when you listen to others.

7. Always work on learning new skills.

8. Tune up before you play.

9. Play with new people. You'll learn new things and make new friends.

10. Have fun!

Bluegrass Word Scramble

Unscramble the letters to form words related to bluegrass music.

(Answers in the back of the book.)

1. o b d o r
2. t e l s i v a f
3. t i r u a g
4. u c s i m
5. e d f i l d
6. n j b o a

7. n a y h o r m
8. o e d l y m
9. l s e b u s g a r
10. r c o d h
11. n n i l d o m a
12. s b s a

Have you Heard the One About .....?

Q: How many guitars does a bluegrass musician need?

A: Just one more

Bluegrass Fitness

The Ultimate Bluegrass Workout

Did you know that playing bluegrass music while sitting down helps a 150-pound guitarist burn 136 calories per hour? Also, if you stand and wear ankle weights, you can increase the calorie burn. Now, put the guitar down and do jumping jacks in between songs while the other pickers are noodling and you'll burn more calories than a tri-athlete.

Run Farther, Train Harder, Get Stronger with Bluegrass Music

Multiple studies indicate that exercise is more fun and more efficient when you listen to music. According to an article in *Scientific American:*

> "Music distracts people from pain and fatigue, elevates mood, increases endurance, reduces perceived effort and may even promote metabolic efficiency. When listening to music, people run farther, bike longer and swim faster than usual—often without realizing it."

Music has even been referred to as a "legal performance enhancing drug." Fast songs with a strong beat produce the best results for exercising. So, forget the slow waltzes and turn up the bluegrass songs with a thumping bass and hot licks, and then start sweating.

Now That's What I Call Marathon Banjo Playing

In 2009, a man ran the Nashville Country Music — 26.2-mile marathon while playing the banjo. He did it as a fundraiser for the Leukemia and Lymphoma Society. He ran the marathon in just over 4 hours.

Test Your Bluegrass Knowledge

How much do you know about bluegrass music? Test your knowledge in this trivia quiz. *(Answers in the back of the book.)*

1. What year did the National Academy of Recording Arts & Sciences award a Grammy for the first time for "Bluegrass Album"?
   a. 1970
   b. 1981
   c. 1985
   d. 1989

2. What was the name of the Bluegrass festival hosted by Bill Monroe?
   a. Bean Blossom
   b. Monroe Fest
   c. World of Bluegrass
   d. Jerusalem Ridge Festival

3. In what state was the above-mentioned festival located?
   a. Kentucky
   b. Tennessee
   c. Indiana
   d. North Carolina

4. Where is the headquarters of the International Bluegrass Music Association?
   a. Nashville, TN
   b. Owensboro, KY
   c. Raleigh, NC
   d. Columbus, GA

5. What bluegrass band performed at the Whitehouse in 1973?
   a. Flatt and Scruggs
   b. The Dillards
   c. Jim and Jessie
   d. Osborne Brothers

6. Who was the first bluegrass group to have a number one song on the country music charts?
   a. Bill Monroe and Blue Grass Boys
   b. Flatt & Scruggs
   c. Osborne Brothers
   d. Alison Krauss & Union Station

Test Your Bluegrass Knowledge (cont.)

7. Which politician played the fiddle and recorded an album with the Country Gentleman?
    a. Sen. Robert Byrd (IN)
    b. Sen. Paul Simon (IL)
    c. Gov. Jerry Brown (CA)
    d. Vice Pres. Al Gore (TN)

8. Pete Kuykendall was a bluegrass musician and was the editor of one of the earliest newsletters to cover strictly bluegrass music. What is the name of the newsletter?
    a. Bluegrass Unlimited
    b. Bluegrass Gazette
    c. Bluegrass Times
    d. Bluegrass News

9. What movie star went to high school with Pete Kuykendall and helped popularize bluegrass music by using the music as a soundtrack for one of his movies?
    a. Steve Martin
    b. Burt Reynolds
    c. Warren Beatty
    d. Clint Eastwood

10. What year was Rocky Top first recorded?
    a. 1964
    b. 1967
    c. 1974
    d. 1976

11. How many frets are there on a standard bluegrass banjo?
    a. 18
    b. 22
    c. 20
    d. 24

12. Which of the following is **NOT** a musical term for a type of scale?
    a. Pentatonic
    b. Diatonic
    c. Ginantonic
    d. Octatonic

Bluegrass vs. Old Timey Music

Old Timey Music has a lot of similarities with bluegrass music, but it also has distinct characteristics. The following information may provide a helpful guide to explain the differences to folks who have just a passing familiarity with the two genres.

- The term "Old Time Music" came into general use in the 1920's. It is also referred to as Old Timey Music, Hillbilly Music and Mountain Music. The term "Bluegrass" didn't come into common use until the 1950's.

- The fiddle is generally the lead instrument in Old Timey music. While Old Timey music emphasizes acoustic string instruments, it is not uncommon for it to include other instruments such as the jug, harmonica, autoharp, jaw harp, concertina, accordion, washboard, spoons, or bones.

- The banjo in an old-timey band is more likely to be an open back banjo played claw-hammer style. Bluegrass bands almost always emphasize the three-finger Scruggs style of banjo playing. (Play it loud!)

- Old Timey musicians play the dulcimer. Bluegrass musicians play the dobro and ask, "What's a dulcimer?".

- Old-timey music is often associated with different types of dancing such as square dancing, contra dancing and clogging. Bluegrass dancing …. generally, is not a thing you want to behold.

- Bluegrass bands take solo breaks from the instruments. In the old-timey style, the instruments typically all play together, all the time, with no breaks or solos.

Bluegrass vs. Old Timey Music (cont.)

- Both old-timey music and bluegrass music are heavily influenced by Appalachian folk music, which in turn was heavily influenced by Old English and Celtic music. Consequently, some songs (such as Soldier's Joy) are commonly played in both genres. Both types of music also draw on gospel, folk, and popular tunes from the early 20th century.

- If you want to start a debate with old-timey musicians, ask an old-time fiddler if the banjo can take the lead at an old-time fiddle convention. If you want to start a debate with a bluegrass musician, ask them to define the term "bluegrass".

- There are regional variations in old-time music. The musical traditions have been preserved and passed along through jams and old-time fiddle conventions. Newly composed tunes are rare in old-time music.

Just Another Banjo Joke

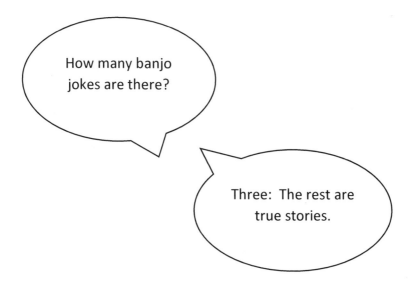

Nine Movies with Banjo Music

(Or ten – but who's counting?)

Banjo songs have been featured in many movie soundtracks. Even though some of the songs in this list are only somewhat bluegrassy, just for fun, how many of these movies have you seen?

	Yes	No	Can't Remember	Who Wants to Know?
O Brother Where Art Thou				
Deliverance				
Zombieland				
Cool Hand Luke				
Muppet Movie				
Bonnie & Clyde				
Cat Ballou				
Cold Mountain				
Smokey and the Bandit				
Song Catcher				

Can you name other movie soundtracks that feature the banjo?

FUN FACT

In <u>Cool Hand Luke</u>, Paul Newman played "Plastic Jesus" on the banjo for a scene in the movie. He insisted on learning how to the play the instrument for filming and delayed completion of the movie by several weeks in order to do so.

Bluegrass Match Game

Everyone gets a sheet of paper and writes down a word(s) to fill in the blanks to these questions.

See which answer gets the most matches.

1. All bluegrass bands should have a _____ player.

2. If you are going to a jam, don't forget your _____.

3. A perfect jam circle is made up of _____ (insert number) of musicians.

4. To learn how to play a new instrument, you should practice _____ hours per week.

5. _____ is my beverage of choice while listening to music.

6. It is completely inappropriate to _____ while sitting in a jam circle.

7. My favorite thing about bluegrass festivals is the _____.

How Well Do You Know Your Train Songs?

Song	Letter Matching the Description
1. Orange Blossom Special	
2. Glendale Train	
3. Wreck of the 97	
4. Wabash Cannonball	
5. Fireball Mail	
6. Greenville Trestle High	
7. John Henry	
8. New River Train	

A. In 1903, this train left Monroe, VA and derailed in Danville, VA.

B. Frank and Jesse James robbed this train in Missouri in 1879.

C. This is a fictional train but there is a river of the same name in Indiana, and both Indiana University and Purdue University marching bands play a song by the same name.

D. This song has the name of a deluxe passenger train that ran between New York City and Miami from 1925 to 1953.

E. This song, about the perils of having multiple lovers, refers to part of the Norfolk and Western system in Virginia.

F. This song was recorded by Doc Watson and written by Jimmy Jett. Both men are from North Carolina. The original title of the song was different from what Doc Watson recorded.

G. This is another fictional train, but the lyrics talk about the freight train being Dallas bound, bound, bound …..

H. This song is about a steel driving man who works by laying track for the railroad. The song is said to be based on a true story, and there is a statue of the man in Talcott, West Virginia.

Best Bluegrass Dog Names

Based on an unscientific poll of dogs tagging along at bluegrass festivals.

Blue – A name for blue-eyed dogs, blue tick hounds, blue heelers and bluegrass dogs.

Banjo – Why not name the dogs "Guitar" or "Dobro"? Don't know. People just like the name Banjo.

Harley – For people who bring their hogs and dogs to bluegrass festivals.

Duke – Uncle Jed's favorite name for a hound dog.

Buddy – Ok. It's not that original - but it is a good name for a bluegrass dog (Better than Fido or Fluffy).

Dooley – Because there is more than one bluegrass song with Dooley in it.

Maggie – Good name for a little dog.

Barkley – For a bluegrass dog that likes to bark at cats.

Millie – For that one-in-a million bluegrass dog.

What is the name of your bluegrass dog(s)?

_____

Practice Tips for Bluegrass Musicians

Below are some key tips that are good advice for any picker.

1. Develop good habits. Always tune your instrument before you start practicing.

2. Try to practice every day, even if it is just 10 to 15 minutes a day. It really helps.

3. Know the lyrics of the song. Even if you don't sing at jams, sing along when you are practicing. It will help you find the melody notes and help with the phrasing of the song.

4. Emphasize the melody notes. It is not just about the notes you play, but the notes you don't play.

5. General guidelines for a one-hour practice session:

    15 minutes – Practice fundamentals. Rolls, scales, licks, hammer-ons, pull-offs….

    15 minutes – Work on the new song you are learning.

    15 minutes – Play the old songs you already know to keep them fresh.

    15 minutes – Noodle. Play around with incorporating new licks into your songs. Find out what works and what doesn't.

6. Know the fretboard so you can move up and down the neck to find melody notes and add variety to your songs. Practice rolls or licks going up and down the neck to build muscle memory and learn what works.

7. Play slowly until you master a technique or song. After you're comfortable playing at a slower pace, you can speed up a notch.

Practice Tips for Bluegrass Musicians (cont.)

8. Practice with a metronome to help you to keep a steady tempo. Practice playing songs at both slow and fast speeds. Even practicing older songs you think you already know pretty well can be done at different tempos.

9. Before you start working on a new song, listen to a recording of the song or to other musicians playing the song at concerts and jam sessions. This will help you internalize the music and learn what the song is supposed to sound like.

10. Set goals for what you want to learn. This will help keep your practice routine on the right track and show you the progress you are making.

11. Practice back-up as well as the leads to songs. Play back-up to recorded songs, and it will help you remember chord progressions and make jamming more fun.

What Is Your Bluegrass Band Name?

So, you and your buddies have started a band. You've been practicing for the last few months, and you have your first gig. Now, you must decide on a name for the band. Don't worry. Just follow the instructions below to find your perfect bluegrass band name.

1. What is the last digit of your phone number? Find the word corresponding to that number on list #1 and write that word in the first blank.

2. What is the mascot/name of your favorite sports team? Write that name in the second blank. (If you don't follow sports, write down your favorite animal.)

3. What is the last digit of the year you were born? Find the word corresponding to that number on list #2 and write that word in the third blank.

The _____ _____ _____ Band

List #1
0. Soggy
1. Crooked
2. Foggy
3. Ramblin
4. Lonesome
5. Grinning
6. Toothless
7. Grumpy
8. Stompin
9. Itchy

List # 2
0. Creek
1. String
2. Valley
3. Mountain
4. Family
5. Fret
6. Canyon
7. River
8. Grass
9. Hillbilly

Bluegrass and Jazz

To bluegrass aficionados, the comparison to a style of music that uses horns, keyboards and percussion may seem a bit of a stretch. There is, however, more in common between the two genres than you may think.

- Both jazz and bluegrass are uniquely American styles of music. Both forms of music are classified as "root music".

- Instrumental pieces feature alternating solos. Typically, one instrument takes the lead and the other instruments play softer to back-up the lead.

- Bluegrass and jazz musicians are both known for enjoying informal jam sessions. At these sessions musicians improvise as they play.

- Both jazz and bluegrass are performed at "festivals" that feature that style of music with multiple stages and workshops.

- Like jazz, the best bluegrass musicians are virtuosos on their instruments.

- Both jazz and bluegrass gained popularity as part of a counter culture movement. In the "Roaring Twenties", jazz was considered avant-garde, while in the 1960's bluegrass was embraced by the anti-establishment folk music crowd.

- Music critics did not immediately embrace either form of music. Initially, music critics considered jazz as mere noise whereas bluegrass was originally regarded as lowly hillbilly music.

- Early jazz recordings from the 1910s to the mid-1920s, use the banjo rather than rhythm guitar. The banjo was loud and could be picked up by early recording technology. During the big band era, however, jazz bands replaced the banjo with the acoustic guitar.

Bluegrass Song Challenge

Pick a word from the list below. Go around the jam circle and everyone must take a turn and name a bluegrass song with that word in the lyric. Whoever is the last person that can name a song, wins.

Word List

Mountain

Home

Blue

Train

Creek

Dog

Variations:

1. Form teams of two to four people each. The team can put their heads together to come up with the name of the song.

2. Each player (or team) must sing a lyric from the song with the word in it.

Did You Know?

- Orville Wright played the mandolin. His mandolin is on display at the Smithsonian National Air and Space Museum in Washington D.C.

- Ricky Skaggs played mandolin on stage with Bill Monroe when he was just a youngster of six years old.

- Ralph Stanley was awarded an honorary Doctorate of Music from Lincoln Memorial University in Harrogate, Tennessee in 1976. He was thereafter known as Dr. Stanley.

- Bill Monroe, Doc Watson and Earl Scruggs all have been inducted into the IBMA Hall of fame as well as received Grammy Lifetime Achievement Awards.

- Jerry Garcia of the Grateful Dead started his music career playing bluegrass. Between 1962 and 1964 he played with a bluegrass band called the "Sleepy Hollow Hog Stompers".

- Hazel Dickens and Alice Gerard released one of the first bluegrass albums by female artists in 1965. (*Who's That Knocking (And Other Bluegrass Country Music)*. The duo was inducted into the IBMA Hall of fame in 2017.

- The dobro gets its name from the Dopyera brothers, John and Emil, who founded the Dobro Manufacturing Company. "Dobro" is a contraction of "Dopyera Brothers". The word also means "goodwill" in their native Slovak and became the company motto - "Dobro means good in any language."

- The tune "Dueling Banjos" was composed in 1955 by Arthur "Guitar Boogie" Smith and was originally called "Feudin' Banjos". The Dillards recorded it as "Duelin Banjos" and played the tune on a 1963 television episode of *The Andy Griffith Show* as part of the role of the Darling Family. The song was made famous by the 1972 film *Deliverance*.

Pick Your Next Jam Song

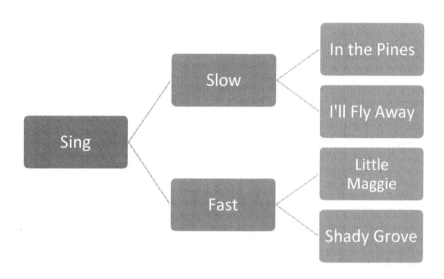

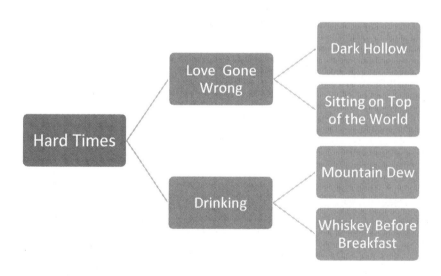

Pick Your Next Jam Song (cont.)

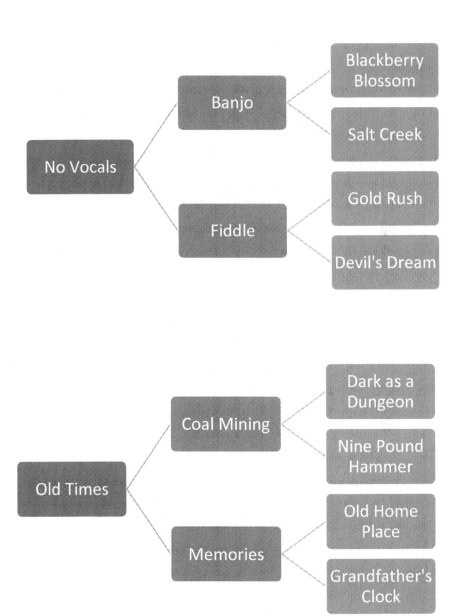

Bluegrass Festival Scavenger Hunt

See how many of these things you can find at a bluegrass festival. Give yourself one point for each thing you find on the list.

1. Person wearing a t-shirt with a picture of a bluegrass instrument on it. (This is an easy one.)

2. A beat-up guitar case without any stickers on it. (This is a hard one.)

3. A jam circle with three mandolin players. (Extra point if there is a dobro player.)

4. A banjo player driving a Porsche. (Wow!)

5. A ball cap with the word "bluegrass" on it. (Another easy one.)

6. A jam circle around a camp fire. (In lieu of a campfire, a grill can count - but only if it is charcoal.)

7. Someone texting or checking their phone in a jam circle. (Party foul.)

8. A bumper sticker with the word "bass" on it. (Extra point if the bass refers to the fish.)

9. A fiddler playing "Faded Love". (Say it isn't so.)

10. A person under the age of ten who is a better picker than you are. (Seriously?)

11. Someone playing a harmonica. (Egads!)

12. Someone at their campsite eating cold leftovers for breakfast. (Yuk!) (Or yum – depending on your point of view.)

13. Someone else with a *Bluegrass Fun Book!* (Yeah!)

Bluegrass Music is Good for You

Music improves academic performance (especially at math).

Playing music relieves stress (especially true of bluegrass music).

Playing music improves social skills (even for banjo players).

Learning music skills provides a sense of achievement.

Don't you forget. Playing an instrument improves memory function.

Music can boost your immune system and reduce pain.

Top Bluegrass Cat Names

Because the cats demanded equal time, here are the top bluegrass cat names.
(Note: Only cat names that start with the letter "M".)

Melody – For cats that purr along with bluegrass music.

Mellifluous – For the pretentious cat. (They actually prefer classical music.)

Max – For the no nonsense bluegrass cat. (Just feed me and let me sleep in the sun.)

Maybelle – In honor of a great lady.

Mando – For bluegrass cats that like to tease bluegrass dogs named Banjo.

Mr. Fiddlehead – Actually, anything that you put after "Mr." will work.

Miss Kitty – For the oh so cute bluegrass cat and Gunsmoke fan.

Mumu – For the Hawaiian cat. (Even though they prefer ukuleles, at least it's still acoustic.)

Add your favorite bluegrass cat name: _____

Guess Who?

Everyone has a piece of paper. Write the answer to each of these questions.

See who in the group gets the most votes.

?? Who in the group is most likely to know the lyrics to the most bluegrass songs?

?? Who in the group is most likely to have fallen asleep at a bluegrass concert?

?? Who in the group is most likely to have been a musical child prodigy?

?? Who in the group is most likely to have a tattoo of a banjo?

?? Who in the group owns the most instruments?

?? Who in the group is the most likely to forget where they parked their car at a bluegrass festival?

?? Who in the group is most likely to have written a funny bluegrass song?

A Day at The Museum

Taking a road trip? Want to learn more about bluegrass music? Below are some museums you might want to include on your itinerary to get that bluegrass fix.

IBMA Museum (Owensboro, KY) – Located in Owensboro, KY on the banks of the Ohio River. Its vision is to be the center for the history and culture of bluegrass. Includes exhibits as well as event space. Check out their web site for upcoming concert dates, workshops and festivals.
http://www.bluegrassmuseum.org/

Grammy Museum (Los Angeles, CA) – Located in downtown Los Angeles. The museum has exhibits on all different kinds of musical genres. Headphones are located throughout the museum and you can listen to samples of various types of music including Bill Monroe, Ralph Stanley and Flatt & Scruggs. Don't miss the film on root music, an original 1948 version of Pete Seeger's "How to Play the 5-String Banjo", or the photo of FDR posing with a bunch of bluegrass musicians.
http://www.grammymuseum.org/

Country Music Hall of Fame and Museum (Nashville, TN) – Where else but Nashville? The museum tells the history of country music, including the common roots of bluegrass and country. Exhibits include Bill Monroe's Mandolin. Performance space for today's artists, including top bluegrass acts.
http://countrymusichalloffame.org/

American Banjo Museum (Oklahoma City, OK) – Really! There is a banjo museum in Oklahoma City. The museum claims to have the largest collection of banjos on public display with over 400 of the instruments. Includes a Hall of Fame, and if you go to the web site you can view the banjo player directory! http://www.americanbanjomuseum.com/

A Day at the Museum (cont.)

Earl Scruggs Center (Shelby, NC) – Housed in the restored historic Cleveland County Courthouse. The Earl Scruggs Center tells the story of native son, Earl Scruggs. It also tells the history and cultural traditions of the region where Earl Scruggs was born and raised and began the three-finger playing style that made him famous. In addition to exhibits, there is event space for rentals and other activities.

Smithsonian (Washington DC) – The Smithsonian Museum has an extensive collection of material (recordings, books, lesson plans, pod casts …..) of roots music including bluegrass. The National Museum of American History has a collection of musical instruments. Visit the web sites at https://folkways.si.edu/ and http://americanhistory.si.edu/

Ellis Island (New York City) – Ellis Island Museum in New York City has a display only on the banjo! Throughout the museum, exhibits describe the many contributions that immigrants have made to the United States, such as their influence on American music. The exhibit features the banjo, originally an African instrument and the accordion, of German origin.

Bill Monroe Museum (Rosine, KY) – Located near Bill Monroe's birthplace, as of 2017, the museum was under construction. Bill Monroe's boyhood home has been restored and is open to the public.
http://www.billmonroemuseum.com/

Banjo Quote

"The ability to play banjo soon places one in position to pick and choose among scores of social invitations. Everywhere the banjoist is assured of a hearty welcome"
(1927 Gibson catalogue).

Bluegrass Words

Believe it or not, you can combine the letters in the word "bluegrass" to make more than 100 other words. Try it and see how many different words you can make.

Hint: Plurals count as a separate word.
(For example: leg, legs - count as two words.)

Now let's get started.

B L U E G R A S S

List words here:

People You Didn't Know that Played the Banjo

1. **President Chester Arthur**

   Chester Alan Arthur was the 21st President of the United States (1881–1885). He assumed the presidency upon the assassination of James A. Garfield and only served the one term. There is a photo of him posing next to a banjo. Although there is not definitive proof that President Arthur actually played the banjo, it is assumed that nobody would pose with this instrument unless they played it or were doing so as part of some 19th century prank. Apparently, he was the only banjo playing president of the United States.

2. **Kirk Douglas**

   He, of the dimpled chin and the star of the movie *Spartacus*, played the tenor banjo in the movie *Man Without a Star*. Rumor has it that he learned to play the banjo under his real name of "Issur Danielovitch", but the name was too hard for banjo players to pronounce. After changing his name to appeal to the banjo crowd, he was discovered and went on to become a Hollywood mega-movie star. All because of the banjo.

3. **Billy Mummy**

   Those of a certain age will remember the child star from the television show *Lost in Space*. For those too young to be familiar with the show, think of it as a cross between *Lost* and *Star Trek*. Billy Mummy played young Will Robinson whose best friend was a robot. Mr. Mummy grew up to become an accomplished musician who plays a number of instruments — including the banjo. His best friend, the robot, grew up to become R2D2's great grandfather.

Bluegrass Bucket List

1. Pick in a bluegrass jam until the sun comes up.

2. Spend the summer festival hopping.

3. Record a CD with bluegrass songs.

4. Share the joy of bluegrass by performing bluegrass music at either a school or a senior center.

5. Host a house party for a bluegrass band.

6. Attend a music camp to improve bluegrass playing skills.

7. Visit a bluegrass historic site or museum.

8. Help a child, grandchild or young person learn to play a bluegrass instrument.

9. Write a bluegrass song.

10. Make your own instrument.

11. What festival, camps, or bluegrass hot spots are on your bucket list?

_____

_____

_____

_____

Bluegrass and Celtic Music

- Bluegrass music is Influenced by the music of Appalachia which has mixed roots in Irish, Scottish and English traditional music.

- Bluegrass includes many fiddle tunes which are derived from old Celtic tunes. Some tunes are known by different names when played in the Celtic genre (i.e. Red Hair Boy, a common bluegrass jam tune is also known as a Celtic tune called "Little Beggarman").

- Fiddle and mandolin are commonly played in both Celtic and Bluegrass music. A banjo is sometimes seen in a Celtic band but is smaller and more similar to an old-time or tenor banjo.

- Celtic music often includes the flutes, pipes, or Irish whistle. Often drumming instruments such as the bodhran from Ireland are also found in Celtic Bands.

- The reels and hornpipes, which are prevalent in bluegrass, have strong connections to Scottish and Irish music. Reels in bluegrass music are typically played at faster tempos than in Celtic bands.

- In Celtic music, informal gatherings of musicians are called a "session". In bluegrass such gatherings are referred to as "jams."

- In Celtic music, vocalists almost always take solo leads. In bluegrass bands, three and four-part harmonies are common.

- Bluegrass musicians generally don't wear kilts, and Celtic musicians generally don't wear overalls.

Bluegrass Charades

Form up to four teams. The player from the first team picks one of the bluegrass song titles below to act out for their teammates. You are not allowed to talk, only act out the title.

Each team has one minute to guess the title. After team #1 is done, the remaining teams take turns with the rest of the songs on the list.

Songs:

Roll in My Sweet Baby Arms

Cripple Creek

Hot Corn, Cold Corn

I'm Walking the Dog

I'll Fly Away

Long Journey Home

Bury Me Beneath the Willow

Bluegrass License Plate Bingo

Next time you are driving to or from a festival, play "Bluegrass Licenses Plate Bingo". Each time you see a license plate from a state, put a checkmark (or "x" if that is your preferred marking) in the state on the map below. At the end of your trip, see how many different state license plates you saw!

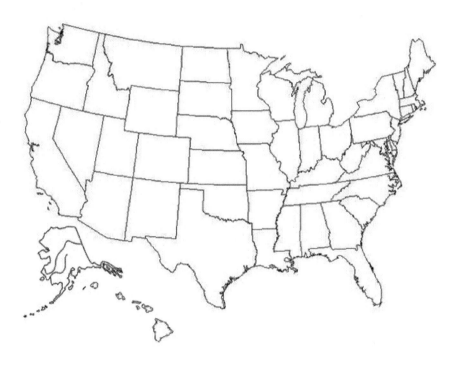

Variation:

On a scale of one to five, rank the license plates on the following scale.

    1 = Very Attractive   2 = Better than Most

    3 = Ho Hum   4 = Ugly

    5 = So Ugly it Would Make an Onion Cry

Promote Bluegrass Music!

1. Join your local bluegrass association.

2. Attend a bluegrass festival or a local bluegrass concert.

3. Support local bluegrass bands by buying their CDs or streaming their songs.

4. Volunteer at a bluegrass festival or concert.

5. Donate an unused instrument or music books to a teacher who can pass them on to the next generation.

6. Read a biography about a bluegrass pioneer. (There are lots of good ones.)

7. Introduce a young person to bluegrass music — bring them to a jam!

8. Sign-up for fiddle camp, banjo camp, mandolin camp, guitar camp, bass camp, or ………..

9. Organize a jam session.

10. Play and listen to bluegrass music!

Make Your Own Banjo Jokes

Have everyone come up with an answer and vote on the funniest one.

Question: How long does it take to tune a banjo?

Answers:

Question: What do you call a roomful of banjo players?

Answers:

Question: What do get when you cross a banjo player with a bass player?

Answers:

Bluegrass Show and Tell

Go around the room and have everyone take a turn to show or tell something from the following list:

1. Identify the favorite sticker on your instrument case and explain how you acquired the sticker.

2. Tell about the first bluegrass festival you attended and who attended the festival with you.

3. Sing your favorite bluegrass song.

4. Tell your favorite banjo joke.

5. Describe your ideal bluegrass road trip.

6. Share your favorite recipe from a bluegrass camp-out.

7. Tell about the funniest thing you have ever seen at a bluegrass festival.

8. Show everyone the latest picture on your smart phone from a bluegrass jam, concert or festival.

9. Tell about the best bluegrass concert you ever attended.

Bluegrass Festival Log

Record the bluegrass festivals you have attended in the log sheet below.

Name	Location	Year(s) Attended

A Year of Bluegrass

January - Happy Bluegrass New Year!

*New Year's Resolution - Practice everyday and learn a new song each month.
*Winter Driving Tip - Make sure you can get to your next jam by keeping your gas tank half full to avoid gas line freeze-up.
*Song of the Month - " Eighth of January"

Feburary - Will You Be My Bluegrass Valentine?

*Take your sweetheart to a bluegrass concert for Valentine's Day.
*Get a deal on a new mattress over Presidents' Day weekend and get a good night of sleep for better pickin & grinnin.
*Song of the Month - "How Mountain Girls Can Love"

March - Top of the Bluegrass Morning to You!

*Play Celtic songs at your Saint Patrick's day jam.
*March is "Change your Strings" month.
*Song of the Month - "Irish Washerwoman"

April - April Showers Bring Bluegrass Flowers

*Watch butterflies while you practice by planting nectar plants in the sunniest areas of the garden to attract these fluttering specimens.
*File your tax returns, or the "tax man" will cometh ("revenuers" in bluegrass lingo).
*Song of the Month - "Wildwood Flower"

May - Bluegrass Mother's Day

*Put on a bluegrass talent show for Mom. Non-musicians can tell banjo jokes or play air guitar.
*Clean out the camper or RV to get ready for festival season.
*Song of the Month - "Mamma Don't Allow"

June - Bluegrass Solstice

*Longest day of the year on June 21 means late night jammin.
*Father's Day - Compile a bluegrass play list for Dad to listen to while driving to festivals.
*Song of the Month - "June Apple"

July - Red, White and Bluegrass

*Before the fireworks, serve watermelon and have a seed spitting contest. (Just don't aim at the pickin circle).
*Use lavendar oil as a natural insect repellent when jammin outside.
*Song of the Month - "Whitehouse Blues"

August - Dog Days of Bluegrass

*Hot sultry dog days of summer are good for a backyard pickin party and BBQ.
*Don't leave your instrument in a hot vehicle. Overheating may cause it to warp or crack (or come unglued).
*Song of the Month - "Salty Dog Blues"

September - Fall into Bluegrass

*September 22 is the fall equinox. If you are jammin at higher latitudes, equinoxes are prime time to see the northern lights.
*Use all of those garden ripe tomatoes to make salsa for your Labor Day jam.
*Song of the Month - "I Ain't Going to Work Tomorrow."

October - Spooky Bluegrass

*In honor of Oktoberfest, serve bratwurst and beer at your next jam.
*Murder ballads and ghostly songs are perfect for a Halloween party set list.
*Song of the Month - "Bringing Mary Home"

November - Thankful for Bluegrass

*Play some bluegrass at the local Veteran's Home (or other nursing home).
*94% of Thanksgiving Day dinners include cranberry sauce. There are no statistics on how many families play bluegrass music after Thanksgiving dinner.
*Song of the Month - "Turkey in the Straw"

December - The 12 Days of Bluegrass

*Tuners, picks, capos or a new set of strings make great stocking stuffers for the special bluegrass musician in your life.
*Make ornaments with photos of favorite bluegrass events from the past year.
*Song of the Month - "Jingle Bells"

Bluegrass Recipe – JAM-balaya

Ingredients

½ green bell pepper (chopped)

1 medium onion (chopped)

2 green onions (chopped)

¼ cup parsley

1 clove crushed garlic

¼ cup butter or margarine

½ lb of smoked andouille sausage (cut up in bite size pieces)

1 box (6 oz) of long grain rice with seasoning mix

1 can chopped stewed tomatoes

½ to 1 lb of cooked shrimp (Salad shrimp or chopped shrimp)

Cajun/Creole seasoning to taste

Directions

1. Sauté bell pepper, onions, garlic and parsley in butter.
2. Add sausage and rice and continue cooking about five minutes
3. Add water and can of tomatoes and seasonings
4. Cover and simmer about 20 minutes, stirring frequently. After rice is cooked, add shrimp and heat through.

Bluegrass Song List

Below is a list of songs mentioned throughout this book. Either check the box for songs you already know how to play/sing or check the box for those songs that you want to learn.

	Songs I know	Songs I want to learn
Ain't Going to Work Tomorrow		
Ballad of Jed Clampett		
Blackberry Blossom		
Blue Moon of Kentucky		
Bluegrass Breakdown		
Bringing Mary Home		
Bury Me Beneath the Willow		
Can't You Hear Me Callin		
Cripple Creek		
Cry, Cry My Darling		
Dark as a Dungeon		
Dark Hollow		
Darling Cory		
Devil's Dream		
Dooley		
Dueling Banjos		
Eighth of January		
Fireball Mail		
Foggy Mountain Breakdown		
Footprints in the Snow		
Glendale Train		
Gold Rush		
Grandfather's Clock		
Greenville Trestle High		
Hot Corn Cold Corn		
How Mountain Girls Can Love		

	Songs I know	Songs I want to learn
I'll Fly Away		
I'm Sitting on Top of the World		
I'm Walking the Dog		
In the Pines		
Irish Washerwoman		
Jingle Bells		
John Henry		
June Apple		
Kentucky Waltz		
Little Georgia Rose		
Little Maggie		
Long Journey Home		
Mama Don't Allow		
Mountain Dew		
Mule Skinner Blues		
My Rose of Old Kentucky		
New River Train		
Nine Pound Hammer		
Old Home Place		
Orange Blossom Special		
Rabbit in the Log		
Red Hair Boy		
Rocky Top		
Roll in My Sweet Baby Arms		
Salt Creek		
Salty Dog Blues		
Shady Grove		
Soldier's Joy		
Toy Heart		
Turkey in the Straw		
Uncle Pen		
Wabash Cannonball		

	Songs I know	Songs I want to learn
Whitehouse Blues		
Wildwood Flower		
Will the Circle be Unbroken		
Whiskey Before Breakfast		
Wreck of the 97		
Add Your Own Songs to the List		

Just for fun, while you are at a festival, if a band (or jam session) plays one of the songs on the list, put a check next to the song. See which songs are the most popular.

Answers

Bluegrass Word Search

Q	S	C	W	E	G	R	L	I	C	K	T
B	Z	B	A	N	D	U	Y	U	I	O	P
R	X	F	T	Y	H	M	I	K	J	A	M
E	F	I	D	D	L	E	O	T	P	L	M
A	A	S	M	O	N	R	O	E	A	T	U
K	B	G	H	N	U	J	M	L	W	R	Y
B	N	L	M	F	E	S	T	I	V	A	L
O	L	L	U	T	R	A	D	O	B	R	O
N	P	O	A	E	S	B	O	E	R	H	B
P	I	M	C	W	G	E	N	R	T	O	A
I	L	U	L	K	I	R	A	M	A	M	N
C	M	S	O	H	T	T	A	R	K	A	J
K	A	I	S	M	B	A	S	S	M	M	O
G	K	C	R	A	L	C	N	O	S	H	A
R	A	D	M	A	N	D	O	L	I	N	y

Answers (cont.)

Bill Monroe Trivia

1. Charlie 2. Rosine, KY 3. 1939 4. Mule Skinner Blues
5. Slim Pickens 6. Stringbean 7. True 8. Kentucky Waltz
9. Lester Flatt 10. True 11. Bill Clinton 12. Footprints in the Snow
14. Sally Ann Forrester 15. King Wilkie

Word Scramble

1. Dobro 2. Festival 3. Guitar 4. Music 5. Fiddle 6. Banjo
7. Harmony 8. Melody 9. Bluegrass 10. Chord 11. Mandolin
12. Bass

Bluegrass Trivia

1. 1989 2. Bean Blossom Festival 3. Indiana
4. Owensboro, KY 5. Osborne Brothers 6. Flatt & Scruggs for "Ballad of Jed Clampett"
7. Sen. Robert Byrd 8. "Bluegrass Unlimited" 9. Warren Beatty in the movie "Bonnie & Clyde"
10. 1967 11. 22 12. Ginantonic

Train Songs

1. D 2. B 3. A 4. C 5. G 6. F 7. H 8. E

About the TriPickaty Academy

The TriPickaty Academy creates specialty publications and products that capture the enthusiasm of devotees of various pursuits. Sharing passions with fellow aficionados enriches the experience and creates good memories. Find your passion and enjoy this and future TriPickaty Academy products.

The initial TriPickaty offerings were developed around the founder's (Kathleen McMahon) passion for bluegrass music and banjo playing. The first part of the academy's name (TriPick), is a salute to the three finger picking style of playing bluegrass banjo while the last part of the name references Kathleen's childhood moniker (Katy).

Visit the TriPickaty Academy web site to find out about other books and products.
tripickaty.com

We are on Facebook!
https://www.facebook.com/TriPickatyAcademy/

Additional copies of the book may be purchased at:
www.amazon.com

The name TriPickaty Academy is trademarked by Applied Communications, LLC

Made in the USA
Columbia, SC
04 May 2018